BOOK 6

Prim-Ed
www.prim-ed.com
Publishing

Grammar minutes

100 minutes to practise and reinforce essential skills

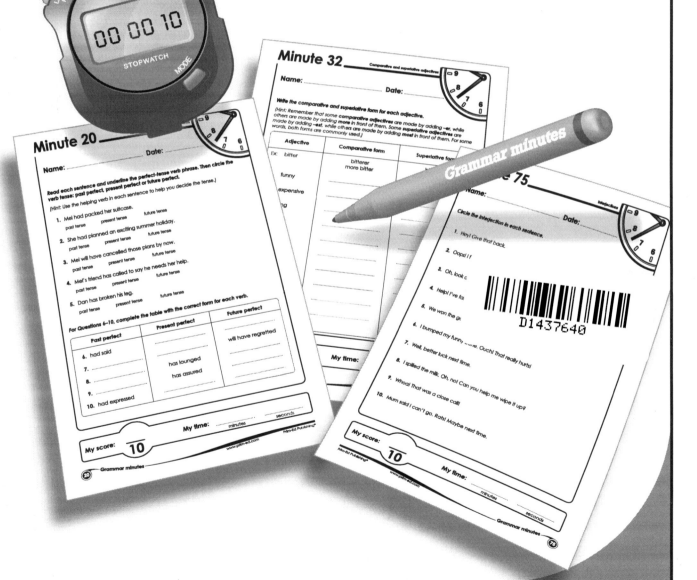

Collene Dobelmann

6332

Grammar minutes *Book 6*

Published by Prim-Ed Publishing® 2011 under licence to Creative Teaching Press.
Copyright© 2009 Creative Teaching Press.
This version copyright©Prim-Ed Publishing® 2011

ISBN 978-1-84654-299-2
PR–6332

Titles available in this series:
Grammar minutes 1
Grammar minutes 2
Grammar minutes 3
Grammar minutes 4
Grammar minutes 5
Grammar minutes 6

Internet websites
In some cases, websites or specific URLs may be recommended. While these are checked and rechecked at the time of publication, the publisher has no control over any subsequent changes which may be made to webpages. It is *strongly* recommended that the class teacher checks *all* URLs before allowing pupils to access them.

View all pages online   **Website:** www.prim-ed.com

GRAMMAR MINUTES – BOOK 6

Foreword

Grammar minutes is a six-book series for primary school pupils, that provides a structured daily programme of easy-to-follow activities in grammar. The main objective is grammar proficiency, attained by teaching pupils to apply grammar skills to answer questions effortlessly and rapidly. The questions in this book provide pupils with practice in the following key areas of grammar instruction:

- *nouns and pronouns*
- *verb forms and verb tenses*
- *adjectives and adverbs*
- *prepositional phrases*
- *contractions*
- *compound and complex sentences*
- *Greek and Latin roots.*

- *word usage*
- *synonyms, antonyms and homophones*
- *noun and pronoun agreement*
- *subject and verb agreement*
- *prefixes/suffixes*
- *appositives and clauses*

Grammar minutes – Book 6 features 100 'minutes', each with 10 classroom-tested problems. Use this comprehensive resource to improve your pupils' overall grammar proficiency, which will promote greater self-confidence in their grammar skills as well as provide the everyday practice necessary to succeed in testing situations. Designed to be implemented in numerical order from 1 to 100, the activities in *Grammar minutes* are developmental through each book and across the series.

Comprehensive teachers notes, record-keeping charts, a scope-and-sequence table (showing when each new concept and skill is introduced), and photocopiable pupil reference materials are also included.

How many minutes does it take to complete a 'grammar minute'?

Pupils will enjoy challenging themselves as they apply their grammar knowledge and understanding to complete a 'grammar minute' in the fastest possible time.

Titles available in this series:

- *Grammar minutes – Book 1*
- *Grammar minutes – Book 2*
- *Grammar minutes – Book 3*
- *Grammar minutes – Book 4*
- *Grammar minutes – Book 5*
- *Grammar minutes – Book 6*

Contents

Teachers notes

How to use this book

Grammar minutes can be used in a variety of ways, such as:

- **a speed test.** As the teacher starts a stopwatch, pupils begin the 'minute'. As each pupil finishes, he/she raises a hand and the teacher calls out the time. The pupil records this time on the appropriate place on the sheet. Alternatively, a particular time can be allocated for the whole class to complete the 'minute' in.
  Pupils record their scores and time on their 'minute journal' (see page vii).

- **a whole-class activity.** Work through the 'minute' together as a teaching or reviewing activity.

- **a warm-up activity.** Use a 'minute' a day as a 'starter' or warm-up activity before the main part of the lesson begins.

- **a homework activity.** If given as a homework activity, it would be most beneficial for the pupils if the 'minute' is corrected and reviewed at the start of the following lesson.

Grammar minutes strategies

Encourage pupils to apply the following strategies to help improve their scores and decrease the time taken to complete the 10 questions.

- To use strategies whenever possible.
- To move quickly down the page, answering the problems they know first.
- To come back to problems they are unsure of, after they have completed all other problems.
- To make educated guesses when they encounter problems they are not familiar with.

A *Grammar minute* pupil activity page.

Name and date
Pupils write their name and the date in the spaces provided.

Questions
There are 10 problems, providing practice in every key area of grammar proficiency.

Score
Pupils record their score out of 10 in the space provided.

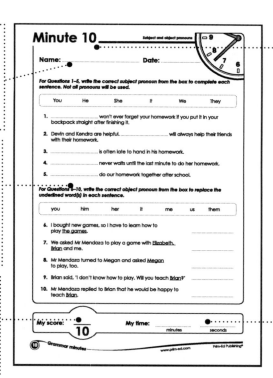

'Grammar minute' number
Grammar minutes are designed to be completed in numerical order.

Time
Pupils record the time taken to complete the 'minute' at the bottom of the sheet. (This is optional.)

Teachers notes

Marking

Answers are provided for all activities. How these activities are marked will vary according to the teacher's organisational policy. Methods could include whole-class checking, partner checking, individual pupil checking, or collection by the teacher.

Diagnosis of problem areas

Grammar minutes provides the teacher with immediate feedback of whole-class and individual pupil understanding. This information is useful for future programming and planning of further opportunities to practise and review the skills and concepts which need addressing.

Make use of the structured nature of the questions to diagnose problem areas; rather than asking who got 10 out of 10, ask the pupils who got Number 1 correct to raise their hands, Number 2, Number 3 etc. In this way, you will be able to quickly determine which concepts are causing problems for the majority of the pupils. Once the routine of *Grammar minutes* is established, the teacher will have time to work with individuals or small groups to assist them with any areas causing problems.

Meeting the needs of individuals

The structure of *Grammar minutes* allows some latitude in the way the books are used; for example, it may be impractical (as well as demoralising for some) for all pupils to be using the same book. It can also be difficult for teachers to manage the range of abilities found in any one classroom, so while pupils may be working at different levels from different books, the familiar structure makes it easier to cope with individual differences. An outline of the suggested age range levels each book is suited to is given on page iii.

Additional resources:

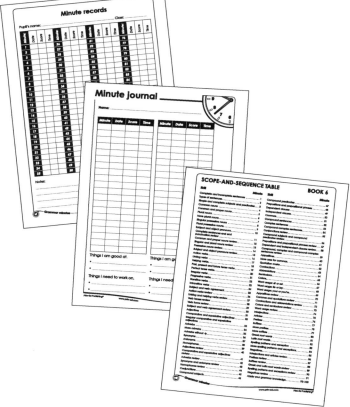

- **Minute records**
  Teachers can record pupil scores and times on the **Minute records** table located on page vi.

- **Scope and sequence**
  The **Scope-and-sequence table** gives the 'minute' in which each new skill and concept appears for the first time.

- **Minute journal**
  Once a 'minute' is completed, pupils record their score and time on their **Minute journal**, located on page vii.

- **Answers to all questions are found on pages 101 to 105.**

Minute records

Pupil's name: .... Class: ....

Minute:	Date	Score	Time	Minute:	Date	Score	Time	Minute:	Date	Score	Time	Minute:	Date	Score	Time
1				26				51				76			
2				27				52				77			
3				28				53				78			
4				29				54				79			
5				30				55				80			
6				31				56				81			
7				32				57				82			
8				33				58				83			
9				34				59				84			
10				35				60				85			
11				36				61				86			
12				37				62				87			
13				38				63				88			
14				39				64				89			
15				40				65				90			
16				41				66				91			
17				42				67				92			
18				43				68				93			
19				44				69				94			
20				45				70				95			
21				46				71				96			
22				47				72				97			
23				48				73				98			
24				49				74				99			
25				50				75				100			

Notes:

....

....

....

....

Minute journal

Name: ....

Minute	Date	Score	Time

Minute	Date	Score	Time

Things I am good at.

• ....

• ....

Things I need to work on.

• ....

• ....

Things I am good at.

• ....

• ....

Things I need to work on.

• ....

• ....

SCOPE-AND-SEQUENCE TABLE   BOOK 6

Name: .... **Date:** ....

Write C *if the sentence is complete or* **I** *if it is incomplete.*

1. Michelle starts at her new school on Friday.   ....

2. Got to get school supplies.   ....

3. Very nervous about the first day.   ....

4. She hopes that she will make friends quickly.   ....

5. Michelle's cousin attends the same school, but they won't have any lessons together.   ....

6. Heard that the history and science classes are hard.   ....

7. Michelle will join the choir as soon as she can.   ....

8. She enjoys singing.   ....

9. Only three more days of summer holidays!   ....

10. Michelle's cousin will show her around the school before the first day.   ....

My score:
$\dfrac{\quad}{10}$

My time: ....
                         minutes   seconds

Minute 2

Name: .... **Date:** ....

Write the correct end punctuation (full stop, question mark or exclamation mark) for each sentence. Then write the type of sentence it is on the line: declarative, interrogative, imperative or exclamatory.

*(Hint: A **declarative** sentence is a statement. An **interrogative** sentence asks a question. An **imperative** sentence makes a request or a command. The 'you' does not appear in the sentence but it is understood. An **exclamatory** sentence shows strong feeling.)*

1. Timothy's first day of school was not bad.......... ....

2. Have you ever been the 'new kid' at school.......... ....

3. I dropped my lunch box. What an embarrassing moment.......... ....

4. I slipped and fell, and my lunch box made a loud clatter.......... ....

5. Did you hurt yourself.......... ....

6. That is how I met my best friend.......... ....

7. She said everyone has moments they would rather forget.......... ....

8. Sit next to me.......... ....

9. I am so ecstatic to finally have a friend.......... ....

10. Tell me your most embarrassing moment.......... ....

My score: ___ **10**

My time: ....
minutes seconds

Name: .... **Date:** ....

For Questions 1–5, circle the simple subject of each sentence. Underline the complete subject.

*(Hint: The **simple subject** is the someone or something the sentence is about. The **complete subject** includes all words related to whom or what the sentence is about.)*

1. Our eager classroom teacher began the lesson.

2. The yellow marker did not show up on the overhead projector.

3. The algebra problem was really difficult to solve.

4. The pupils, including my best friend, have an English lesson after maths.

5. Do you have PE today?

For Questions 6–10, circle the simple predicate for each sentence. Underline the complete predicate.

*(Hint: The **simple predicate** is the action or linking verb without any other words that modify it or describe the subject. The **complete predicate** includes all words that show what the complete subject is or does.)*

6. Ms Linette asked Tyson to demonstrate how to solve the problem.

7. I solved the problem by working backwards.

8. My two classmates were the only ones to correctly answer the problem.

9. Several members of the class tried to work through the problem again.

10. Did anyone use a different method?

My score: $\dfrac{}{10}$

My time: ....
minutes   seconds

Name: .... **Date:** ....

Circle the two common nouns in each sentence.

1. Dylan and Shelby bought a puppy yesterday from the pound.

2. They can't think of a good name for their pet.

3. Shelby wanted to name the dog 'Bubbles' and get its collar engraved.

4. Dylan and Shelby got into an argument over their choices.

5. He thought of naming the puppy 'Bear' because it looks like a bear.

6. Shelby did not want to get into a fight, but she disliked his suggestion.

7. Finally, their mother offered an alternative.

8. How about solving the problem by calling the hyperactive creature 'Dash'?

9. 'He does love to play chasey', the kids noted.

10. Dylan and Shelby called to their new friend, who came running with his tail wagging.

My score: _____

10

My time: ....

minutes   seconds

Minute 5

Name: .... Date: ....

Circle the common noun(s) in each sentence. Underline any proper nouns that are missing capitalisation and rewrite them correctly on the lines.
The number in brackets tells how many nouns in total you should circle or rewrite in each sentence.

1. My dog, remy, has a shaggy coat. (3)   ....

2. I had to take Remy to see his groomer at
   furry friends grooming shop. (5)   ....

3. He bathes Remy and brushes his fur. (1)   ....

4. Another worker, henry, clips Remy's claws
   and cleans his ears. (4)   ....

5. Remy likes to play with his friend, trixie. (2)   ....

6. She wears a pink collar around her neck. (2)   ....

7. Henry rewards the dogs with treats for good
   behaviour. (3)   ....

8. The dogs lick Henry's hands and face
   enthusiastically. (3)   ....

9. Then the canines are ready to go home. (2)   ....

10. If you have a pet, take it to the shop on
    highland street. (4)   ....

My score: __ 10 __   **My time:** ....
                                              minutes   seconds

Minute 6 _____

Name: .... **Date:** ....

Circle the two plural nouns in each sentence.

1. Our cat had its babies on a bed of blankets yesterday.

2. Mum says our house has more pets than people.

3. She asked her coworkers and friends if any of them wanted a kitten.

4. Sandra said her twins have always wanted cats.

5. I found families for three more of the felines.

6. The kitten with orange and white patches, the grey kitten and the white kitten still need homes.

7. She likes to settle on her haunches and then pounce at your toes when you least expect it!

8. Her favourite games are chasing my neighbour's puppy and playing with the leaves in the garden.

9. Luckily, my neighbours kept the orange and white kitten, and two women took the last two.

10. If I had two wishes, I would get to keep a kitten, and Mum would get us dogs!

My score: _____
10

My time: ....
minutes   seconds

Minute 7

Name: .... **Date:** ....

Write the plural form for each noun.

1. church   ....

2. tree   ....

3. country   ....

4. bus   ....

5. baby   ....

6. deer   ....

7. shelf   ....

8. goose   ....

9. belief   ....

10. child   ....

My score: $\dfrac{}{10}$ **My time:** ....
                                                 minutes   seconds

Minute 8

Name: .... Date: ....

Write the singular possessive form to replace the underlined phrase in each sentence.

*(Hint: A **singular possessive noun** shows ownership by one person or thing. Adding 's to a noun makes it possessive.)*

1. The <u>toy that belongs to the dog</u> is under the sofa.

   ....

2. Please give me the <u>bottle that belongs to the baby</u>.

   ....

3. Do you have <u>the ball that belongs to Trevor</u>?

   ....

4. The <u>stinger of the bee</u> is sharp!

   ....

5. The <u>tail of the puppy</u> wagged and wagged.

   ....

6. The <u>wing of the bird</u> is not broken.

   ....

7. I like <u>the car that belongs to your mother</u>.

   ....

8. The <u>back tyre of the bus</u> was flat.

   ....

9. The <u>tracks of that deer</u> led to the garden.

   ....

10. Have you seen <u>the new haircut of Mum</u>?

    ....

My score: _____

10

My time: ....
          minutes   seconds

Minute 9

Name: .... **Date:** ....

Write the plural possessive form to replace the underlined phrase in each sentence.

*(Hint: A **plural possessive noun** shows ownership by more than one person or thing. When a plural noun ends in **-s**, adding an apostrophe ['] to the end makes it possessive. Example: The room belonging to the sisters = sisters' room.)*

1. The <u>uniforms that belong to the cheerleaders</u> are red and white.

   ....

2. The <u>helmets that belong to the bicycle riders</u> keep them safe.

   ....

3. The <u>horns that belong to the trumpeters</u> sound great.

   ....

4. Do you like the <u>performances of the marching bands</u>?

   ....

5. I can hear the <u>cheers of the people</u>.

   ....

6. The <u>coaches of the teams</u> are excited about the game.

   ....

7. The <u>uniforms of the mascots</u> are hot and itchy.

   ....

8. The food tent sells <u>cakes and pies made by the football parents</u>.

   ....

9. When it rains, it's hard to see over the <u>umbrellas belonging to the fans</u>.

   ....

10. The <u>taunts of the rivals</u> are all in good fun. ....

My score: $\dfrac{}{10}$

My time: ....
minutes   seconds

Minute 10

Name: .... Date: ....

For Questions 1–5, write the correct subject pronoun from the box to complete each sentence. Not all pronouns will be used.

You	He	She	It	We	They

1. .... won't ever forget your homework if you put it in your backpack straight after finishing it.

2. Devin and Kendra are helpful. .... will always help their friends with their homework.

3. .... is often late to hand in his homework.

4. .... never waits until the last minute to do her homework.

5. .... do our homework together after school.

For Questions 6–10, write the correct object pronoun from the box to replace the underlined word(s) in each sentence.

you	him	her	it	me	us	them

6. I bought new games, so I have to learn how to play <u>the games</u>. ....

7. We asked Mr Mendoza to play a game with <u>Elizabeth, Brian</u> and me. ....

8. Mr Mendoza turned to Megan and asked <u>Megan</u> to play, too. ....

9. Brian said, 'I don't know how to play. Will you teach <u>Brian</u>?' ....

10. Mr Mendoza replied to Brian that he would be happy to teach <u>Brian</u>. ....

My score: 10 / 10

My time: ....
minutes   seconds

Complete sentences and end punctuation review

Name: .... **Date:** ....

Read each sentence. If the sentence is incomplete, write I. If the sentence is complete, add the correct end punctuation mark.

1. Where would you like to spend your holiday..........

2. Love to go to Newquay, Cornwall..........

3. I have heard that the beaches are beautiful..........

4. I can't wait to learn to surf..........

5. My brothers and I have before..........

6. I bought goggles and snorkels..........

7. Are you comfortable in the water..........

8. Yes, I like to swim..........

9. When do you want to..........

10. Is it time to pack yet..........

My score: _____

10

My time: ....
        minutes   seconds

Minute 12

Name: .... Date: ....

Underline the common noun(s) and circle any proper noun(s) in each sentence. The number in brackets tells how many total nouns you should underline or circle.

1. Stephen visited the United States capital, Washington, DC, last winter. (5)

2. He met his grandfather and his cousin, Joseph, there. (3)

3. They visited the Washington Monument and the Lincoln Memorial. (2)

4. Papa Joe wanted to visit the Vietnam Veterans Memorial. (2)

5. They could see the dome of the United States Capitol from the National Mall. (3)

6. Stephen attends Gallaudet University in the city. (3)

7. Stephen and Joseph chatted excitedly as they walked along Pennsylvania Avenue. (3)

8. They took photos of the White House but did not see the president. (3)

9. Stephen had bought a small souvenir flag of the United States. (3)

10. Joseph bought postcards of the Oval Office and the *USS Philadelphia*. (4)

My score: _____
10

My time: ....
                minutes   seconds

Minute 13

Name: .... Date: ....

Write the singular or plural form for each noun.

Singular	Plural
1. person	....
2. cherry	....
3.	cactuses or cacti
4. industry	....
5.	sheep
6.	scarves
7. woman	....
8. vertebra	....
9.	parentheses
10. calf	....

My score: $\overline{10}$

My time: ....
                                    minutes   seconds

Minute 14 —————

Name: .... **Date:** ....

For Questions 1–5, circle singular possessive or plural possessive to describe the underlined words in each sentence.

1. The <u>islanders' boats</u> were long, slender rowboats.

   singular possessive   plural possessive

2. That <u>boat's markings</u> are different from the others.

   singular possessive   plural possessive

3. All the other <u>boats' paintings</u> are similar.

   singular possessive   plural possessive

4. A <u>man's voice</u> calls to the oarsmen.

   singular possessive   plural possessive

5. The <u>oarsmen's response</u> comes back loud and strong.

   singular possessive   plural possessive

For Questions 6–10, write the plural possessive form for each phrase.

Singular possessive	Plural possessive
6. man's oars	....
7. island's shore	....
8. person's net	....
9. tribe's custom	....
10. wave's crest	....

My score: ——— **10**

My time: ....
                minutes   seconds

Name: .... **Date:** ....

Write the correct pronoun from the box to replace the underlined noun in each sentence.

she	we	they	him	us

1. It's Dad's birthday. Mum bought <u>Dad</u> a new watch. ....

2. Our car broke down. Will you take <u>Keith and me</u> to school? ....

3. <u>Hannah</u> makes her own jewellery. ....

4. Our neighbours left, but <u>the neighbours</u> are coming back soon. ....

5. <u>My brothers and I</u> are throwing a party for my mother. ....

Write the correct pronoun from the box to complete each sentence. Use each pronoun only once.

you	I	it	he	them

6. Trey and Toni like sweets, so we brought .... some chocolate.

7. .... look like you have seen a ghost!

8. The gardeners who were searching for the rabbit finally noticed .... near the tree.

9. .... brought him some of my homemade chicken soup.

10. .... got in trouble for hitting his sister.

My score:

$\dfrac{}{10}$

My time: ....
                                   minutes   seconds

Minute 16

Name: .... **Date:** ....

Write your own action verbs to complete the paragraph. Use each verb only once.

Victoria wants to .... a pie for dessert. Victoria

           1.

.... a list of groceries to buy. She puts the list in her purse and

           2.

.... to the shop. She .... tart apples and

           3.   4.

.... the flour, cinnamon and sugar. Victoria ....

           5.   6.

her items to the checkout. She .... home immediately and

                              7.

.... her work space. She carefully measures the ingredients. She

           8.

.... the recipe closely. Victoria's family .... the

           9.   10.

pie with ice-cream and savours every bite!

1. ....   6. ....

2. ....   7. ....

3. ....   8. ....

4. ....   9. ....

5. ....   10. ....

My score: _____
10

My time: ....
                minutes   seconds

www.prim-ed.com   Prim-Ed Publishing®

Name: .... **Date:** ....

Circle the linking verb in each sentence.

*(Hint: A **linking verb** does not express action. It connects the subject to the rest of the information about the subject.)*

1. Abel was sick on Friday.

2. He became queasy after lunch.

3. Ms Grey said, 'Abel, you seem feverish'.

4. 'I feel awful', he whispered.

5. 'I am sorry!' responded Ms Grey.

6. She added, 'You'll be more comfortable in the first aid room.

7. She and Abel's classmates were helpful.

8. The first aider told Abel, 'Your mother is concerned. She'll pick you up soon'.

9. 'You are kind', said Abel.

10. 'You'll feel well by Monday', said the first aider.

My score: _____

10

My time: ....
minutes   seconds

Minute 18

Name: .... **Date:** ....

Circle the helping verb in each sentence.

*(Hint: A **helping verb** is used with another verb and expresses such things as person, number, mood, or tense.)*

1. I am reading *Tuck everlasting* by Natalie Babbitt.

2. My friends are reading it with me.

3. We have enjoyed it so far.

4. The main character, Winnie, is trying to decide if she wants to live forever.

5. My friends wondered what they might do in her situation.

6. I was thinking about the same thing.

7. I will ask my teacher if she thinks it is a good idea.

8. I think I would choose to live forever.

9. My teacher does agree with me.

10. She has pondered the question, too.

My score: _____

10

My time: ....
minutes   seconds

Minute 19

Name: .... Date: ....

Read each sentence and underline the verb or verb phrase. Then circle the verb tense: past tense, present tense, or future tense.

1. I do different chores every day after school.

    past tense   present tense   future tense

2. Yesterday, I cleaned the rabbit's cage.

    past tense   present tense   future tense

3. I also helped Mum with dinner.

    past tense   present tense   future tense

4. Rene will help with the cooking tonight.

    past tense   present tense   future tense

5. She and Mum plan to make spaghetti and meatballs.

    past tense   present tense   future tense

6. I will water the lawn and the pot plants.

    past tense   present tense   future tense

7. I forgot to sweep the patio.

    past tense   present tense   future tense

8. I try to remember to take out the rubbish.

    past tense   present tense   future tense

9. I will get my pocket money on Friday if all my chores are done.

    past tense   present tense   future tense

10. I save half of my pocket money for holidays.

    past tense   present tense   future tense

My score: ____
10

My time: ....
             minutes   seconds

Minute 20

Name: .... **Date:** ....

Read each sentence and underline the perfect-tense verb phrase. Then circle the verb tense: past perfect, present perfect or future perfect.

(Hint: Use the helping verb in each sentence to help you decide the tense.)

1. Mel had packed her suitcase.

   past tense   present tense   future tense

2. She had planned an exciting summer holiday.

   past tense   present tense   future tense

3. Mel will have cancelled those plans by now.

   past tense   present tense   future tense

4. Mel's friend has called to say he needs her help.

   past tense   present tense   future tense

5. Dan has broken his leg.

   past tense   present tense   future tense

For Questions 6–10, complete the table with the correct form for each verb.

Past perfect	Present perfect	Future perfect
6. had said	....	....
7.	....	will have regretted
8.	has lounged	....
9.	has assured	....
10. had expressed	....	....

My score: _____
10

My time: ....
                minutes   seconds

www.prim-ed.com   Prim-Ed Publishing®

Minute 21

Name: .... **Date:** ....

Write the correct form for each verb to complete the table.

(Hint: **Irregular verbs** do not end in **–ed** in the past or past participle tenses.)

Present tense	Past tense	Past participle
1. eat	....	eaten
2.	bit	bitten
3. forget	forgot	....
4. break	....	broken
5. write	wrote	....
6.	bled	bled
7. undo	....	undone
8. spread	spread	....
9.	felt	felt
10. give	gave	....

My score: $\dfrac{\quad}{10}$

My time: .... minutes .... seconds

Minute 22

Name: .... Date: ....

For Questions 1–5, read each sentence, and underline the progressive verb phrase. Then circle the verb tense: **past progressive**, **present progressive** or **future progressive**.

(Hint: Use the helping verb in each sentence to help you decide the tense.)

1. We are expecting a large crowd for the family reunion.

   past progressive   present progressive   future progressive

2. My cousins and their parents are staying at our house for a week.

   past progressive   present progressive   future progressive

3. Mum and Aunt Anna were planning the itinerary.

   past progressive   present progressive   future progressive

4. They will be entertaining many out-of-town guests.

   past progressive   present progressive   future progressive

5. Dad was encouraging me to organise a talent show for the children.

   past progressive   present progressive   future progressive

For Questions 6–10, write the present progressive form to replace each underlined verb phrase.

6. I <u>was thinking</u> that a play of our family history would be a better idea.   ....

7. Cousin Greg <u>will be helping</u> me write and direct it.   ....

8. They <u>will be creating</u> the set and costumes.   ....

9. Dad <u>was saying</u> how this is a good idea.   ....

10. I <u>will be looking</u> forward to the festivities!   ....

My score: ———
10

My time: ....
                 minutes   seconds

Name: ....   **Date:** ....

Read each sentence and underline the transitive verb. Then draw an arrow from the transitive verb to its object.

(Hint: A **transitive verb** is an action verb that requires the use of a direct object to answer **whom**? or **what**? Example: The judge underline{sentenced} the man to three years in prison.)

1. Tana loves her grandparents.

2. They know many things.

3. Grandpa collects coins.

4. He tells the history behind each one.

5. He also builds miniature sailboats.

6. On Sunday, he showed his latest masterpiece to Tana.

7. Grandma writes delightful poetry for children.

8. She sends her verses to all her children and grandchildren.

9. They enjoy reading them aloud to each other.

10. Tana memorises her favourite rhymes.

My score: 10   **My time:** .... minutes   .... seconds

Minute 24

Name: ....   Date: ....

Read each sentence and underline the intransitive verb or verbs. If the sentence contains a word or phrase in bold type, circle the question it answers about the verb: **how, where or when.**

1. The hurricane winds blew **loud and fast**.

    how   where   when

2. Hannah hid **in the shower**.

    how   where   when

3. The trees creaked and moaned.

    how   where   when

4. Windows rattled.

    how   where   when

5. The rain fell **constantly** for five hours.

    how   where   when

6. The storm **finally** died.

    how   where   when

7. It ended **around noon**.

    how   where   when

8. Hannah went **outside**.

    how   where   when

9. She stepped **carefully** over the debris.

    how   where   when

10. Hannah and her neighbours gathered **on the footpath**.

    how   where   when

My score: _____
10

My time: ....
            minutes   seconds

Name: .... **Date:** ....

Circle the verb that correctly completes each sentence.

1. Tony (doesn't/don't) like chocolate cake.

2. However, our brothers and my mother (love/loves) it.

3. They always (order/orders) chocolate cake for dessert at restaurants.

4. Tony (ask/asks) for cheesecake with fruit.

5. He usually (do/does) not finish it, though.

6. Mum (eat/eats) the leftovers.

7. Dad, Lisa and Mum (prefer/prefers) chocolate cake.

8. Mum says it isn't good to eat until you (is/are) stuffed.

9. Dad does not listen, and he (do/does) it anyway.

10. Mum just (shake/shakes) her head.

My score: ___ ___

10

My time: ....
minutes   seconds

Minute 26

Name: ....   **Date:** ....

Find all of the action verbs in the box. Write them on the lines below.

read	travel	be	by	listen
poor	am	save	gather	breathe
eat	best	breath	full	were
pupil	think	recognise	dance	funny

1. ....

2. ....

3. ....

4. ....

5. ....

6. ....

7. ....

8. ....

9. ....

10. ....

My score: $\dfrac{\quad}{10}$

My time: ....
minutes   seconds

Name: .... Date: ....

Read each sentence and underline the verbs or verb phrases. Then circle the verb form for each sentence: helping *or* linking.

1. Chris became irritated with his disobedient dog.

    helping   linking

2. He was trying to teach it tricks.

    helping   linking

3. I was watching them.

    helping   linking

4. Boxer was unruly and hyperactive from the beginning.

    helping   linking

5. He was running away from Chris.

    helping   linking

6. Chris felt very frustrated.

    helping   linking

7. Boxer was more and more uncooperative.

    helping   linking

8. Both Chris and Boxer were hoping for a break.

    helping   linking

9. Chris and I were relaxing on the patio.

    helping   linking

10. Boxer was finally calm.

    helping   linking

My score: ___/10   **My time:** ....
minutes   seconds

Minute 28

Name: .... Date: ....

Write the correct verb or verb phrase to complete the table.

Present	Past perfect	Present perfect	Future perfect
1.	had swum	have swum	will have swum
2. crawl	....	have crawled	will have crawled
3.	had drunk	have drunk	will have drunk
4. break	....	have broken	will have broken
5. grow	had grown	....	will have grown
6. walk	had walked	have walked	....
7. fall	....	have fallen	will have fallen
8. hit	had hit	....	will have hit
9. grab	had grabbed	have grabbed	....
10. crush	....	have crushed	will have crushed

My score: ———
10

My time: ....
minutes   seconds

www.prim-ed.com   Prim-Ed Publishing®

Name: .... Date: ....

Circle the verb form—transitive or intransitive—for each sentence below.

1. Tom joined the theatre arts club.   transitive   intransitive

2. He acts quite well.   transitive   intransitive

3. Tom's audition began shakily.   transitive   intransitive

4. He got the lead role in the school play.   transitive   intransitive

5. He memorised his lines in no time.   transitive   intransitive

6. He practised each scene.   transitive   intransitive

7. They rehearsed every day.   transitive   intransitive

8. The theatre teacher directed the rehearsals.   transitive   intransitive

9. Opening night went smoothly.   transitive   intransitive

10. The audience cheered wildly.   transitive   intransitive

My score: ___ 10

My time: ....
minutes   seconds

Minute 30

Name: .... **Date:** ....

Write the correct verb form to complete each sentence.

1. Tina and her sister .... late on Saturday mornings.

   sleep   sleeps

2. Her mother doesn't even .... to wake them up.

   try   tries

3. When Tina finally .... up, she is grouchy.

   get   gets

4. She .... not a morning person.

   is   are

5. Tina and her mother .... breakfast quietly.

   eat   eats

6. Tina .... more cheerful and awake.

   feel   feels

7. After breakfast, they .... their day.

   plan   plans

8. Tina .... an idea.

   have   has

9. Tina and her sister .... to go to the amusement park.

   want   wants

10. They .... going to have a great time.

   is   are

My score: ⎯⎯
10

My time: ....

minutes   seconds

Minute 31

Name: .... Date: ....

Circle each adjective. Then draw an arrow from the adjective to the noun it describes. The number in brackets at the end of the sentence tells how many examples you will find.

1. We took a trip to the spectacular zoo in London. (1)

2. The sunny weather made for a beautiful day. (2)

3. The first animals we visited were the scaly reptiles. (2)

4. Then we saw giant elephants. (1)

5. Did you know that elephants are hairy? (1)

6. We walked into a warm hut filled with tropical plants. (2)

7. The hut housed loose hummingbirds. (1)

8. We watched the busy birds drink sugary nectar. (2)

9. The large cats are a favourite sight. (2)

10. I like to watch the playful cubs. (1)

My score: ___ / 10

My time: .... minutes .... seconds

Minute 32

Name: .... **Date:** ....

Write the comparative and superlative form for each adjective.

*(Hint: Remember that some **comparative adjectives** are made by adding **–er**, while others are made by adding **more** in front of them. Some **superlative adjectives** are made by adding **–est**, while others are made by adding **most** in front of them. For some words, both forms are commonly used.)*

	Adjective	Comparative form	Superlative form
Ex:	bitter	bitterer more bitter	bitterest most bitter
1.	funny	....	....
2.	expensive	....	....
3.	long	....	....
4.	sick	....	....
5.	small	....	....
6.	quick	....	....
7.	exciting	....	....
8.	hot	....	....
9.	colourful	....	....
10.	pretty	....	....

My score: ———
$\frac{}{10}$

My time: ....
minutes   seconds

www.prim-ed.com   Prim-Ed Publishing®

Minute 33

Name: .... Date: ....

Write the comparative and superlative forms for each irregular adjective.

(Hint: A few adjectives are considered irregular because they are written as entirely different words in the comparative and superlative forms.

Adjective	Comparative	Superlative
good	1.	2. ....
bad	3.	4. ....
far	5.	6. ....
much	7.	8. ....
little	9.	10. ....

My score: $\dfrac{}{10}$

My time: ....
minutes   seconds

Minute 34

Name: .... **Date:** ....

Rewrite each adjective as an adverb. Then write the adverb and the verb it modifies as a phrase.

*(Hint: An **adverb** is a word that tells **how, when** or **where** something happens.)*

Adjective	Adverb	Verb	Adverbial phrase
Ex: proud	proudly	stood	proudly stood
1. bold	....	walked	....
2. calm	....	spoke	....
3. excited	....	shout	....
4. nervous	....	wait	....
5. loud	....	bark	....
6. easy	....	pass	....
7. quick	....	heals	....
8. complete	....	finishes	....
9. busy	....	prepares	....
10. brave	....	jumps	....

My score: $\dfrac{}{10}$ **My time:** ....

minutes   seconds

Name: .... **Date:** ....

Circle the adverb in each sentence. Then draw an arrow from the adverb to the verb it modifies.

*(Hint: An **adverb** is a word that tells **how**, **when** or **where** something happens.)*

1. Leah happily agreed to play tennis with her sister.

2. Andrea serves the ball fiercely.

3. The ball flies swiftly over the net.

4. Leah reacts speedily to meet the ball.

5. She soundly hits the ball with her racquet.

6. Andrea barely misses the ball.

7. When it is Leah's turn to serve, she swings wildly.

8. Andrea returns the ball expertly.

9. The girls' skills are closely matched.

10. Andrea and Leah will gladly return to the tennis court.

My score: ___

10

My time: ....

minutes   seconds

Name: .... **Date:** ....

Circle the adverb in each sentence. Then draw an arrow from the adverb to the verb it modifies.

*(Hint: An **adverb** is a word that tells **how**, **when** or **where** something happens.)*

1. Noeline always coaches the junior softball team.

2. The players are young, but they work hard to please her.

3. Melanie catches every ball that comes near her.

4. Out of everyone, Michelle runs the fastest.

5. Cheryl hits the ball the furthest.

6. Noeline shouted often during the last game.

7. She pointed and yelled, 'Throw the ball there!'

8. The ball buzzed close to the ground, but Melanie caught it.

9. Noeline's team won again.

10. 'You have done well!' Noeline congratulated her players.

My score: _____
10

My time: ....
minutes   seconds

Name: .... **Date:** ....

Draw a line from each word to its synonym.

1. damp   imitate

2. avoid   ignore

3. stop   grasp

4. definite   faithful

5. grab   angry

6. copy   challenge

7. loyal   moist

8. furious   discontinue

9. dare   perplex

10. baffle   certain

My score: $\frac{}{10}$ **My time:** ....
                                              minutes   seconds

Minute 38

Name: .... **Date:** ....

Draw a line from each word to its antonym.

1. drenched   busy

2. bright   dead

3. seize   dull

4. alive   awake

5. complex   simple

6. hefty   smooth

7. seldom   give

8. asleep   dry

9. coarse   often

10. idle   light

My score: _____   **My time:** ....
           10   minutes   seconds

Minute 39

Name: .... **Date:** ....

Write a homophone for each word.

*(Hint: **Homophones** sound the same but mean different things and are spelt differently.)*

1. right   ....

2. through   ....

3. here   ....

4. meet   ....

5. seam   ....

6. hair   ....

7. bear   ....

8. dear   ....

9. steel   ....

10. roll   ....

My score: $\dfrac{}{10}$

My time: ....
               minutes   seconds

Minute 40

Name: .... Date: ....

For Questions 1–3, circle the word that correctly completes each sentence.

1. An adjective modifies a (noun, verb).

2. A (comparative, superlative) adjective compares or contrasts two things.

3. A (comparative, superlative) adjective compares or contrasts three or more things.

For Questions 4–10, write the adjectives from the box that correctly complete the paragraph. Use each adjective only once.

> helpful   better   undefeated   quick   shaky   advanced   winning

Rose is a .... football player than I am. She has ....
                          4.   5.

reflexes. Unfortunately, at first my passing skills were .... However,
                                                                                    6.

Rose is a .... coach. I am a more .... player since
                          7.   8.

she has worked with me. I even scored the .... goal at our last
                                                                        9.

match. Our team is now ....
                                          10.

4. ....   8. ....

5. ....   9. ....

6. ....   10. ....

7. ....

My score: _____   My time: ....
              10   minutes   seconds

Name: .... Date: ....

For Questions 1–5, circle the correct comparative or superlative adjective to complete each sentence.

1. Janelle is the (shorter/more shorter) of the two girls.

2. After two days of being sick, Matthew felt (worse/more bad) than ever.

3. Brian and Jason have curly hair, but Fred's is the (curliest/most curliest).

4. She felt (more lonelier/lonelier) at night during her week at camp.

5. This stationery has (cuter/more cute) designs.

For Questions 6–10, write the comparative and superlative forms of each adjective.

Adjective	Comparative form	Superlative form
6. big	....	....
7. little	....	....
8. much	....	....
9. sleepy	....	....
10. good	....	....

My score: __ 10

My time: ....
minutes   seconds

Minute 42

Name: .... **Date:** ....

Circle the adverb in each sentence. Then draw an arrow from the adverb to the verb or verb phrase it modifies.

1. Ted and Mario always go camping in March.

2. It usually rains in April.

3. 'Let's pitch our tent here', Ted said.

4. 'No, let's camp closer to the stream', Mario answered.

5. They waited patiently for their dinner.

6. Mario deftly cleaned the fish.

7. Ted carefully lit a fire to cook them.

8. They ate happily and then went to sleep.

9. In the morning, they hiked up the mountain cautiously.

10. They leisurely admired the view from the top.

My score:
10

My time: ....
minutes   seconds

Name: .... **Date:** ....

Read each pair of words. Write S if they are synonyms or A if they are antonyms.

1. loyal, devoted ....

2. alive, dead ....

3. imitate, mimic ....

4. constantly, never ....

5. identical, unlike ....

6. complex, straightforward ....

7. avoid, ignore ....

8. halt, cease ....

9. humorous, comical ....

10. relaxed, tense ....

My score: $\dfrac{}{10}$

My time: ....
       minutes   seconds

Minute 44

Name: .... **Date:** ....

Write the correct homophone from the box to complete each sentence.

to/too/two	sea/see	flour/flower
your/you're	there/they're/their	needed/kneaded
weather/whether	pale/pail	wood/would
piece/peace		

1. The child took his shovel and his .... to the beach to build sandcastles.

2. The .... was sunny and perfect.

3. The family ate a picnic lunch right .... on the beach.

4. The seagulls wanted some lunch, ...

5. He pretended to make bread and added .... to his mixture.

6. He .... the pretend dough.

7. 'Would you like a .... of bread?' he asked.

8. 'I ....', replied his mother.

9. 'Seth, ... a good baker!' she said.

10. They pretended to eat, and then they swam in the ....

My score: $\dfrac{}{10}$

My time: ....
  minutes   seconds

Name: .... **Date:** ....

Circle the correct conjunction to complete each sentence.

*(Hint: A **conjunction** is a word that joins words or groups of words. It can show togetherness or contrast.)*

1. Rafael wanted to join the hockey team; (however/since/or), his mother thought it was too dangerous.

2. He borrowed his friend's uniform (and/so/because) she could see the protective pads he would wear.

3. Rafael (yet/or/and) Dad convinced his mother to go to a practice.

4. They knew it could help change her mind, (because/or/and) it might convince her she was right.

5. Rafael's mother saw that the boys played hard, (although/but/also) the coaches supervised them well.

6. She said Rafael could join the team, (since/except/because) he had to promise to be careful.

7. Rafael didn't know whether to jump for joy (but/and/or) nod seriously.

8. Rafael's mother had relented, (because/or/yet) she was still worried about his safety.

9. Rafael is an excellent defender, (so/or/because) he made the team.

10. Rafael's mother (but/yet/and) father went to every game.

My score: ___ **10**

My time: ....
minutes   seconds

Name: .... **Date:** ....

*For each sentence, underline the compound subject. If a sentence does not have a compound subject, write **None** on the line.*

*(Hint: A **compound subject** has two or more simple subjects with the same predicate.)*

1. Annie visits Sandy's Ice-cream Shop every Friday. ....

2. She and her friends love to go there after school. ....

3. Lemon custard and butter pecan are her two favourite flavours. ....

4. Chocolate sprinkles, walnuts or chocolate chips make great toppings. ....

5. Annie likes them all. ....

6. She orders something different each time she goes there. ....

7. Sandy lets Annie sample new flavours and new toppings before ordering them. ....

8. Sundaes and milkshakes are also popular treats. ....

9. Annie and Sandy have become friends. ....

10. Sandy told Annie she could work at the ice-cream shop when she is old enough. ....

My score: _____

10

My time: ....
minutes   seconds

Name: .... **Date:** ....

*For each sentence, circle the compound predicate's verbs. If a sentence does not have compound predicate verbs, write **None** on the line.*

1. Jenny tumbles and dives competitively.   ....

2. She dreams of competing at the Olympics and
   believes one day she will.   ....

3. She trains very hard at both sports.   ....

4. Jenny thinks hard and ponders which sport to
   stick with.   ....

5. Her training sessions are long and hard.   ....

6. Jenny and her mother feel she can't possibly keep
   doing both.   ....

7. Jenny's schoolwork gets more difficult each year.   ....

8. Her coaches have been supportive and have
   worked around her schedule.   ....

9. Jenny's parents are not rushing her decision.   ....

10. They encourage her and tell her to take her time.   ....

My score: $\dfrac{}{10}$ **My time:** ....

minutes   seconds

Minute 48

Name: .... **Date:** ....

For Questions 1–5, circle the preposition in each group of words.

1. red   before   earlier

2. after   previously   stay

3. during   quietly   very

4. near   set   yesterday

5. to   how   two

For Questions 6–10, circle the prepositional phrase in each sentence.

6. The cat spotted a squirrel in the garden and decided to try to catch it.

7. It chased the squirrel across the grass.

8. They ran between the houses where I could barely see them.

9. The speedy squirrel escaped into the alley.

10. It turned the corner, ran up a telephone pole, and disappeared.

My score: _____
10

My time: ....
minutes   seconds

Minute 49

Name: .... **Date:** ....

For Questions 1–5, circle the five dependent clauses in the box.

*(Hint: A **dependent clause** does not express a complete thought and is not a complete sentence on its own.)*

> when the cake was served
>
> she came home at last
>
> if you need my opinion
>
> because I was tired
>
> that slobbery dog pants
>
> and if I remember correctly
>
> until the police arrived

For Questions 6–10, underline the dependent clause in each sentence.

6. My friend, who does not have a dog, loves to play with mine.

7. I don't know what happened yesterday.

8. Wherever Mason goes, he is loved.

9. If you agree to help, I won't forget it.

10. The cat that has the white patches is mine.

My score:

10

My time: ....
minutes   seconds

Name: .... **Date:** ....

For Questions 1–5, circle the five independent clauses in the box.

*(Hint: An **independent clause** expresses a complete thought and could stand alone as its own sentence.)*

after supper

I know Mr Fletcher

because she was ill

Maria is a postal worker

please pass the potatoes

the sun came up

carry the boxes

For Questions 6–10, underline the independent clause in each sentence.

6. Thomas is a veterinarian who makes house calls.

7. They care for animals more than most people.

8. With skilled expertise, they help sick pets.

9. People count on them to make their animals well.

10. I want to be like them when I grow up.

My score: ___ / **10**

My time: ....
minutes   seconds

Name: .... **Date:** ....

Insert the missing commas in each sentence.

1. Even though Ralph and Linda are siblings they get along pretty well.

2. Their television preferences differ so they try to compromise when deciding what to watch.

3. Ralph likes to watch comedies talk shows and action shows but Linda likes dramas detective shows and game shows.

4. Sometimes they argue but the fight never lasts long.

5. Their parents usually don't have to get involved although that used to happen a lot.

6. They would shout at each other and they were so loud the neighbours could hear them.

7. This embarrassed their parents so they taught Ralph and Linda how to be cooperative with one another.

8. Ralph and Linda composed a schedule of who decided what to watch and it worked.

9. They based the schedule on favourite shows but each person ended up having to sacrifice one or two shows.

10. Their parents were happy and the neighbours were relieved.

My score:
___
10

My time: ....
                minutes   seconds

Name: .... **Date:** ....

For each sentence, write Yes *if it is a compound sentence* or No *if it is not.*

*(Hint: A **compound sentence** has more than one independent clause, which are often joined by a conjunction.)*

1. Katy's holiday to Hawaii was splendid. ....

2. She took tours of Oahu, Maui and Kauai. ....

3. Visiting three islands was exhausting, but she loved every minute of it. ....

4. The favourite part of her trip was swimming with dolphins. ....

5. The gentle creatures snickered and they seemed to invite her to play. ....

6. The marine biologist taught the visitors about dolphin behaviour, so Katy listened carefully. ....

7. Dolphins are very intelligent, social creatures. ....

8. Katy did not see any hair on the dolphins, so she was surprised to learn they are mammals. ....

9. The dolphins easily entertained the crowd, and the dolphins looked happy as well. ....

10. Katy is thinking she might like to become a marine biologist one day. ....

My score: _____

10

My time: ....

minutes   seconds

Name: .... **Date:** ....

For each sentence, write Yes if it is a complex sentence or No if it is not.

*(Hint: A **complex sentence** combines an independent clause with one or more dependent clauses.)*

1. My sister's hamster was very sick. ....

2. When I saw how sad Andrea was, I wanted to help. ....

3. I took Minnie to the veterinarian, even though I don't like hamsters. ....

4. After examining Minnie, Dr Rains gave her some medicine. ....

5. Dr Rains gave me more medicine to take home for Minnie. ....

6. I gave Minnie the medicine because Andrea couldn't administer it properly. ....

7. Before we knew it, she was running on her exercise wheel. ....

8. When Minnie began to perk up, Andrea perked up, too. ....

9. She made a thank-you card for me. ....

10. It made me happy, and I was glad that I helped. ....

My score: ___
10

My time: ....
minutes   seconds

Minute 54

Name: .... Date: ....

Underline both independent clauses in each compound-complex sentence.

1. Giovanna joined the school band, but Selma, who was more athletic, joined the basketball team.

2. Giovanna thought that Selma was making a mistake, but Selma, who is usually indecisive, was sure of her decision.

3. The girls were sad not to be in the same classes, but they both looked forward to new experiences because they spent all their time together.

4. From the start of the school year, the girls barely saw each other, and they missed their close friendship.

5. They got together at weekends, and they talked about everything that came to mind.

6. Giovanna and Selma supported each other, but they didn't agree about all things, like which extracurricular activity to join.

7. Even though the girls didn't see each other often, they remained friends and they introduced one another to new people.

8. Giovanna and Selma were both hard workers, and they excelled at their talents, which made their parents proud.

9. Giovanna, who had joined the drum section, played at Selma's basketball games, and the crowd loved it.

10. The beat sparked energy in the team, so they played better when the drum section was there.

My score: _____

10

My time: ....
minutes   seconds

Name: .... **Date:** ....

For Questions 1–5, write five conjunctions from the box on the lines below.

always	but	because	very	so	however	yours	and	up

1. ....

2. ....

3. ....

4. ....

5. ....

For Questions 6–10, circle the conjunction in each sentence.

6. Matthew wanted to be an astronaut, but he had poor maths skills.

7. He had to do something or he would fall too far behind in class to catch up.

8. His mother took him to a tutor so Matthew would get more individual instruction.

9. Matthew's tutor was firm, yet he was very helpful.

10. Matthew's maths began to improve, and his confidence soared.

My score:

10

My time: ....

minutes   seconds

Minute 56

Name: .... **Date:** ....

Circle either compound subject *or* compound predicate *to describe each sentence.*

*(Hint: A **compound subject** has two or more simple subjects with the same predicate. A **compound predicate** has two or more predicates sharing the same subject.)*

1. Hawaii was built by volcanoes and still continues to grow through volcanic activity.

   compound subject   compound predicate

2. Hawaii became a US state in 1959 and is a lovely holiday spot.

   compound subject   compound predicate

3. Culture and traditions are very important to native Hawaiian people.

   compound subject   compound predicate

4. Tourists are greeted with 'Aloha!' and receive flower leis.

   compound subject   compound predicate

5. Kauai and Maui are popular islands to visit.

   compound subject   compound predicate

6. Honolulu is densely populated and serves as the islands' capital city.

   compound subject   compound predicate

7. Citizens of Hawaii and many visitors fight to preserve the natural beauty of the islands.

   compound subject   compound predicate

8. Endangered sea turtles and other marine life swim free in Hawaii's waters.

   compound subject   compound predicate

9. Lava erupts from Kilauea Volcano and flows to the sea.

   compound subject   compound predicate

10. The beautiful scenery and gentle weather make for a balmy paradise.

    compound subject   compound predicate

My score: ____ **10**   **My time:** ....
                                                      minutes   seconds

www.prim-ed.com   Prim-Ed Publishing®

Minute 57

Prepositions and prepositional phrases review

Name: .... **Date:** ....

For Questions 1–5, write the correct preposition from the box to complete each sentence. Use each preposition only once.

inside	behind	before	near	after

1. It's never a good idea to hide .... a car.

2. It's not a good idea to swim straight .... you eat.

3. Children should never play .... an open flame.

4. Never leave your pet .... a hot car.

5. Always look both ways .... crossing the street.

For Questions 6–10, write your own prepositional phrase to complete each sentence.

6. The children walked ....

7. Their playhouse was located ....

8. Two girls leant ....

9. They talked ....

10. They felt safe ....

My score: _____
10

My time: ....
minutes   seconds

Name: .... **Date:** ....

Circle either **dependent clause** *or* **independent clause** *to describe the underlined words in each sentence.*

1. Alaska entered the Union in 1959 <u>as the 49th state</u>.

   dependent clause   independent clause

2. Alaska is separated from the United States by Canada, <u>and it is more than twice the size of Texas</u>.

   dependent clause   independent clause

3. <u>Juneau is Alaska's state capital</u>, but Anchorage is the most populous city.

   dependent clause   independent clause

4. <u>If you would like to visit Juneau</u>, you would have to fly or go by ship.

   dependent clause   independent clause

5. <u>Alaska has many islands</u>, so it has many kilometres of shoreline.

   dependent clause   independent clause

6. In summer, daytime temperatures range from 15 °C to 32 °C, <u>so they vary greatly</u>.

   dependent clause   independent clause

7. <u>If you visit Anchorage in autumn</u>, you might see the northern lights.

   dependent clause   independent clause

8. The average winter temperature there is about –9 °C, <u>so you would have to bundle up!</u>

   dependent clause   independent clause

9. <u>Alaska is home to Mount McKinley</u>, the highest point in North America.

   dependent clause   independent clause

10. Sled dogs, <u>which are often mixed breeds</u>, pull heavy loads and people through harsh climates.

    dependent clause   independent clause

My score: ___ **10**   **My time:** .... minutes .... seconds

Name: .... **Date:** ....

For Questions 1–5, write dependent clause(s) or independent clause(s) to correctly complete each sentence.

1. A compound sentence joins two ....

2.–3. A complex sentence has one .... and

   one or more ....

4.–5. A compound-complex sentence joins two or more

   .... and one or more

   ....

For Questions 6–10, read each sentence, and circle whether it is compound, complex or compound-complex.

6. Gymnastics is a difficult sport, and it requires excellent coordination and balance.

   (a)   compound   (b)   complex   (c)   compound-complex

7. The apparatus on which gymnasts compete are different for men than they are for women.

   (a)   compound   (b)   complex   (c)   compound-complex

8. Both men and women do the floor and vault exercises, but all the other events are different.

   (a)   compound   (b)   complex   (c)   compound-complex

9. The balance beam, which Rena thinks is the most difficult apparatus, is 10 cm wide, and it stands 125 cm high.

   (a)   compound   (b)   complex   (c)   compound-complex

10. Tom finds the pommel horse most challenging, so he trains very hard to improve his skills on it.

   (a)   compound   (b)   complex   (c)   compound-complex

My score: _____

10

My time: ....
                minutes   seconds

Minute 60

9
8
7
6

Name: .... **Date:** ....

Circle the appositive phrase in each sentence.

*(Hint: An **appositive** identifies or renames the words before it. Example: Our teachers, **Mr Jones and Ms Liddell**, went to a conference on Friday.)*

1. Mount Everest, the mountain with the highest altitude in the world, is located in the Himalayan Mountain Range.

2. Mount Everest is about 29 029 feet, or 8848 metres, above sea level.

3. Sir Edmund Hillary, one of the first men to climb Mount Everest, received his knighthood for his spectacular achievement.

4. Junko Tabei, a Japanese mountain climber, was the first woman to scale Mount Everest.

5. Summiting, or reaching the top of a mountain, gives mountain climbers a tremendous sense of satisfaction.

6. Avalanches cause most of the fatalities, or deaths, among mountain climbers on Mount Everest.

7. Mauna Kea, an inactive volcano in Hawaii, is actually taller than Mount Everest when the portion below sea level is included in the measurement.

8. K2, the second highest mountain on earth, measures 8611 metres above sea level.

9. The mountain in North America that has the highest peak above sea level, Mount McKinley, is located in Alaska.

10. Mount McKinley is 20 320 feet, or 6193.6 metres, above sea level.

My score: _____
10

My time: ....
            minutes   seconds

www.prim-ed.com   Prim-Ed Publishing®

Name: .... **Date:** ....

For each sentence, insert the missing commas in the correct places.

1. Ren was born on Monday 15 June 1998.

2. He wants to eat pizza go bowling and open presents on his birthday.

3. On his last birthday he had a swimming party.

4. It had been a hot humid day.

5. You were at Ren's party weren't you?

6. Ren's father said 'Ren you remember to thank your guests for coming'.

7. Ren answered 'Don't worry Dad!'

8. Ren wishes to go to Anaheim California on his birthday.

9. He says 'Celebrating at Disneyland would be great fun!'

10. For now he will be content with sticking close to home.

My score: _____

10

My time: ....
minutes   seconds

Name: .... **Date:** ....

Insert the missing quotation marks for each sentence. If the sentence does not need quotation marks, write None on the line.

1. Have you ever seen a manatee? I asked Don. ....

2. He said that he had not. ....

3. I told him that they were large marine mammals that are shaped like seals. ....

4. Oh! he exclaimed. I have read about them. ....

5. Don't they usually live in warm, tropical waters? he asked. ....

6. Yes, but manatees are endangered, I answered. ....

7. Don informed me that many weigh over 450 kilograms. ....

8. I read that they are sometimes called sea cows, Don added. ....

9. Ben lives in Australia, and he sees them sometimes, I said. ....

10. What other marine life is endangered? Don asked. ....

My score: _____
10

My time: ....
minutes   seconds

Name: .... **Date:** ....

Circle the two words in each sentence that can be combined to form a contraction. Write the contraction on the line.

1. Earlier, they were out, but they are at home now.

....

2. Mr Hoff told him that he should have studied more.

....

3. You will be disappointed.

....

4. It is almost the holidays!

....

5. Either I can pick up the food or we will eat in.

....

6. On holidays, they would take the train to the beach.

....

7. She does not have a train pass.

....

8. 'Do not leave without me!'

....

9. Sunflowers and tulips are not in season.

....

10. You have finished already?

....

My score: _____
10

My time: ....
minutes   seconds

Minute 64

Name: .... **Date:** ....

For each sentence, circle the title or address word and write its abbreviation on the line.

1. I shop at Mister Gregorino's shop.   ....

2. His father, General Joseph Gregorino, opened the shop
    after he left the army in 1924.   ....

3. The shop will be passed on to George Gregorino Junior
    when he is ready.   ....

4. They asked Senator Miller to give them advice.   ....

5. I need to see my dermatologist, Doctor Sykes, for this rash. ....

6. Captain Pullman stood on deck, surveying the ocean.   ....

7. I used to live by Marty's Drycleaners on Hepburn Avenue.   ....

8. The closest junction for Marty's is High Street.   ....

9. Turn left onto Linden Road.   ....

10. Brocken Lane is on the right.   ....

My score: ___
  10

My time: ....
                 minutes   seconds

Minute 65

Name: .... **Date:** ....

For each sentence, insert the missing semicolon in the correct place.

1. Seth and Victor were in an accident however, they were not injured.

2. Jesse was the only actor who memorised the lines therefore, he got the lead role.

3. I should not have slipped then I might have won the race.

4. Corey got bucked off his horse however, he got right back on.

5. My dog, Matilda, loves to ride in the car therefore, I take her everywhere dogs are allowed.

6. Janice thought the critics were wrong to criticise her play indeed, they simply did not understand it.

7. Martine didn't think anyone noticed her mistake besides, she didn't care if they did.

8. Mr Lee was an excellent teacher however, his pupils thought he was strict.

9. Tiffany learned to drive on a deserted country road indeed, it had been located in the middle of nowhere.

10. Rhode Island is the smallest state in the United States however, it has the longest official name: 'State of Rhode Island and the Providence Plantations'.

My score: ____
10

My time: ....
minutes   seconds

Minute 66

Name: .... Date: ....

For Questions 1–3, write a word from the box to correctly complete each sentence.

closing	dialogue	appositive	before	list	action

1. When summarising, a colon is used .... the summary.

2. A colon used after the sentence *Use the following ingredients* signals

   a ....

3. In plays, colons follow names to signal ....

For Questions 4–10, insert the missing colon in the correct place.

4. The bread recipe calls for four ingredients yeast, water, flour and salt.

5. *Jason* Hi, Kathleen! I've been looking for you everywhere.

6. Let me make the following suggestions first, take notes; second, ask questions; and third, review your notes after the lecture.

7. Sir We met at the Mytown Chamber of Commerce Meeting last week.

8. Please bring the following supplies scissors, glue, map, pencils and a rubber.

9. To Whom it May Concern I am writing in response to the job advertisement in The Chronicle.

10. Send the cheque to the following address 227 Montgomery Avenue, Mytown.

My score: 10

My time: ....
   minutes   seconds

Minute 67

Name: .... **Date:** ....

*Write **sit** or **set** to complete each sentence.*

1. Please .... your drink on the coaster.

2. Come and .... and talk to me for a while.

3. The sun has always .... in the west.

4. Daisy, ... the books on the table.

5. My dog has not yet learnt to ....

6. My grandmother does not like to .... for long periods of time.

7. Mother asked her to .... the table for dinner.

8. We .... at the table to eat dinner.

9. .... the groceries on the counter before you drop the bags!

10. The vase will be .... on the mantle to decorate the room.

My score: ___ / 10

My time: .... minutes .... seconds

Name: .... **Date:** ....

Write lie *or* lay *to complete each sentence.*

1. I will .... my cards on the table for you.

2. I asked if I could .... down in the nurse's office.

3. Don't .... the matches where they will get damp.

4. Will you .... the baby in his crib?

5. The child was sick and could do nothing but .... in bed.

6. When I feel lazy, I just .... on the couch and watch television.

7. What does it feel like to .... on a waterbed?

8. I will .... the letters on the desk for you.

9. My dogs, Shaggy and Trevor, ... in the sun.

10. I .... my bag on the chair.

My score: _____
10

My time: ....
minutes   seconds

Name: .... **Date:** ....

Write your or you're to complete each sentence.

1. I hope .... going to come to the party.

2. .... parents said they would pick you up at 8 o'clock.

3. They will use .... brother's car.

4. Bring .... favourite music to the party.

5. .... a great singer.

6. .... friends would love to hear you sing a song.

7. Do .... nerves bother you when you perform?

8. What do you do while .... waiting to go on stage?

9. All of .... hard work and constant practising has paid off.

10. I'll be sure that .... singing at my next party.

My score: $\dfrac{}{10}$

My time: ....
minutes   seconds

Minute 70

Name: .... **Date:** ....

Underline the appositive phrase in each sentence.

(Hint: Check the remaining words—they should still form a sentence that makes sense.)

1. London, the capital of England, is located in the south-east.

2. Canberra, the capital of Australia, is a great place to visit.

3. Macchu Pichu, often called 'The Lost City of the Incas', was built some 2430 metres above sea level.

4. Bouvet Island, the world's most remote island, is in the South Atlantic Ocean.

5. Juneau, Alaska's capital city, is the most remotely located capital city in the United States.

6. The state capital of Queensland, the Sunshine State, is Brisbane.

7. Dublin, the capital of the Republic of Ireland, is home to the rock band U2.

8. Wellington, the capital of New Zealand, is located on the southern tip of North Island.

9. The Eiffel Tower is found in Paris, the capital of France.

10. Western Australia, which occupies one-third of the continent, is half as large again as the US state of Alaska.

My score: _____
10

My time: ....
minutes   seconds

Name: .... **Date:** ....

Insert commas and quotation marks in the correct places to complete each sentence.

1. What type of books do you like to read? Mrs Turner asked me.

2. I like to read mysteries historical fiction and poetry I replied.

3. She said that I could borrow her books and she helped me choose the first one.

4. It was a fictional story about a girl who lived in Dover England during World War II.

5. When I was finished with it I asked Mrs Turner May I borrow another?

6. She replied Of course you may.

7. Carlie you should keep a journal and write notes about all the books you read Mrs Turner suggested.

8. I wrote in a journal every night and soon I began to have ideas about stories I could write.

9. The more I wrote the stronger my writing became.

10. I enjoy reading and writing more than ever now thanks to Mrs Turner.

My score: ____
10

My time: ....
            minutes   seconds

Name: .... **Date:** ....

For Questions 1–5, underline the two words in each sentence that can be combined to form a contraction. Write the contraction on the line.

1. We are ready to leave school. ....

2. Raise your hand if you are going on the bus today. ....

3. Although the weather bureau said it was going to be cold, it is sunny and warm. ....

4. She could have had two biscuits, but she only took one. ....

5. Laura and I said that we would go to the shop to pick up the milk. ....

For Questions 6–10, write the full word for each abbreviation.

6. Capt. ....

7. Sen. ....

8. St ....

9. Mr ....

10. Ave ....

My score: **10**   **My time:** ....
                                              minutes   seconds

Name: .... **Date:** ....

For Questions 1–5, write C for colon or S for semicolon to tell what punctuation mark should be used in each example.

1. After a name to show dialogue in a play   ....

2. To set off a list of items   ....

3. To join two independent clauses   ....

4. Before words such as *therefore*, *however* and *besides*   ....

5. Instead of a full stop to introduce a series of related sentences   ....

For Questions 6–10, insert either a colon or a semicolon in each sentence.

6. I should have worked late then I would have finished the project.

7. I need these things from the grocer eggs, milk, butter and yoghurt.

8. Please send the package to this address 1999 Hummingbird Lane, Yourtown.

9. Leila was the only brave one therefore, they all followed her lead.

10. Follow these steps first, glue the pom-pom onto the craft sticks; second, secure the pipe-cleaners in place; third, add the stickers for eyes.

My score: _____

10

My time: ....
                                                      minutes   seconds

Name: .... **Date:** ....

Circle the word that best completes each sentence.

1. .... desk is always neater than mine.
   Your You're

2. Your pencils .... neatly in your pencil box.
        lie   lay

3. You always .... your books in your desk in a tidy stack.
       sit   set

4. .... always prepared because your supplies are organised.
   Your You're

5. Maybe if I .... next to you, I will learn better organisational skills.
      sit   set

6. It's frustrating to never know where I have .... my things.
             sit   set

7. Will you help me organise my desk like .... desk?
           your you're

8. You can .... back and relax on that sofa while you tell me
      lie   lay

   what to do.

9. .... a helpful person.
   Your You're

10. When I .... down to sleep tonight, I will give thanks that you
       lie   lay

    helped me.

My score: $\dfrac{\quad}{10}$ **My time:** ....
                 minutes   seconds

Name: .... **Date:** ....

Circle the interjection in each sentence.

1. Hey! Give that back.

2. Oops! I forgot my homework.

3. Oh, look at that cute puppy!

4. Help! I've fallen and I can't get up!

5. We won the game! Hooray!

6. I bumped my funny bone. Ouch! That really hurts!

7. Well, better luck next time.

8. I spilled the milk. Oh, no! Can you help me wipe it up?

9. Whoa! That was a close call!

10. Mum said I can't go. Rats! Maybe next time.

My score: ____
10

My time: ....
minutes .... seconds

Name: .... **Date:** ....

Complete each sentence with the correct article: a, an or the.

1. Every day after school, I go with Mum to get .... baby from daycare.

2. Then some days we go to the grocery shop with .... list of items we need.

3. 'Please go and get .... fruit, while I get the other things', Mum says.

4. At the checkout, we realise we forgot .... milk.

5. I hurry to the back of the shop to grab .... litre of milk.

6. Sometimes, I need a snack, so I'll eat .... apple on the way home.

7. Every Friday, Mum starts to prepare pasta as soon as we get home. It makes

   .... irresistible meal.

8. Morgan, ... baby, is not old enough to enjoy it yet.

9. Mum sometimes feeds her .... jar of mashed carrots.

10. Her face is .... amusing sight when it's smeared with sticky, orange food.

My score: _____

10

My time: ....
minutes   seconds

Name: .... **Date:** ....

Add a prefix from the box to change the meaning of the word. You may use a prefix more than once.

| dis | un | ir | retro | anti | micro | non | multi |

Base word	Prefix	New word
1. assemble	....	....
2. sense	....	....
3. active	....	....
4. attractive	....	....
5. cultural	....	....
6. wave	....	....
7. reversible	....	....
8. dairy	....	....
9. bacterial	....	....
10. certain	....	....

My score:

10

My time: ....

minutes   seconds

Minute 78

Name: .... **Date:** ....

Rewrite each base word with the given suffix.

(Hint: Watch out for spelling changes!)

Base word	Suffix	New word
1. kind	-ness	....
2. happy	-ness	....
3. weary	-ness	....
4. soft	-ness	....
5. empty	-ness	....
6. intend	-tion	....
7. attend	-tion	....
8. subtract	-tion	....
9. elect	-tion	....
10. create	-tion	....

My score: $\overline{10}$

My time: ....
minutes   seconds

Minute 79

Name: .... **Date:** ....

Rewrite each base word with the given prefix. You may use a prefix more than once.

in	semi	im	auto	re	pre	de

Base word	Prefix	New word
1. direct	....	....
2. test	....	....
3. appear	....	....
4. circle	....	....
5. graph	....	....
6. form	....	....
7. mobile	....	....
8. caution	....	....
9. possible	....	....
10. decisive	....	....

My score: ___ / **10**

My time: .... minutes .... seconds

Name: .... **Date:** ....

Rewrite each base word with the given suffix.

(Hint: Watch out for spelling changes!)

Base word	Suffix	New word
1. fold	-able	....
2. wash	-able	....
3. erase	-able	....
4. move	-able	....
5. like	-able	....
6. hope	-less	....
7. fear	-less	....
8. sense	-less	....
9. friend	-less	....
10. care	-less	....

My score: $\dfrac{}{10}$ **My time:** ....
                                                   minutes   seconds

Name: .... **Date:** ....

Draw a line from the Greek root word to its meaning. Draw another line from the meaning to the sample word.

Root word	Meaning	English word
1. dia	distance	podiatrist
2. pod	time	metric
3. chrono	foot	epidermis
4. gen	skin	bibliography
5. hydro	water	chronology
6. tele	book	hydrate
7. meter	life	telescope
8. biblio	through or across	diagonal
9. bio	measure	generation
10. derm	birth	biology

My score: ___
10

My time: ....
minutes   seconds

Name: .... **Date:** ....

Draw a line from the Latin root word to its meaning. Draw another line from the meaning to the sample word.

Root word	Meaning	English word
1. sol	plant	aquarium
2. aqua	right	affix
3. cred	write	inscribe
4. herb	water	pedicure
5. pedi	sun	territory
6. terra	fasten	incredible
7. fix	belief	construct
8. scrib	build	justice
9. just	feet	solar
10. struct	earth	herbivore

My score: ___

10

My time: ....

minutes   seconds

Minute 83

Name: .... **Date:** ....

Write C for each word if it is spelt correctly. If the word is spelt incorrectly, write the correct spelling on the line.

1. friend   ....

2. recieve   ....

3. sieze   ....

4. beleive   ....

5. neighbour   ....

6. retreive   ....

7. either   ....

8. wierd   ....

9. eerie   ....

10. field   ....

My score: ‾‾‾‾‾ **10**

My time: ....
                                         minutes   seconds

Minute 84

Name: .... Date: ....

Write **C** for each word if it is spelt correctly. If the word is spelt incorrectly, write the correct spelling on the line.

1. monkies ....

2. flies ....

3. ladies ....

4. babies ....

5. fries ....

6. turkies ....

7. holidays ....

8. cries ....

9. chimnies ....

10. journies ....

My score: ___10___

My time: ....
minutes   seconds

www.prim-ed.com   Prim-Ed Publishing®

Minute 85

Name: .... **Date:** ....

For Questions 1–5, write the words that signal negatives.

no	barely	always	nowhere	everywhere
either	nobody	any	all	neither

1. ....

2. ....

3. ....

4. ....

5. ....

For Questions 6–10, write C next to the sentence if it uses the negatives correctly. If the sentence uses the negative incorrectly, write I.

6. I didn't buy no Halloween sweets for trick-or-treaters yet. ....

7. My brother does not want to wear a costume this year. ....

8. I can't barely wait to wear my ghoulish costume! ....

9. My little sister doesn't like it none. ....

10. Nobody helped me make the costume. ....

My score:
10

My time: ....
minutes   seconds

Minute 86

Name: .... Date: ....

For Questions 1–5, write an interjection before each sentence.

1. ....! Do you have the time?

2. ....! I sprained my ankle!

3. ...., we will do better next time.

4. ....! I left my grocery list at home.

5. ...., what an adorable creature!

For Questions 6–10, write the correct article, a, an or the, before each group of words.

6. .... great pyramids of Giza

7. .... sheet of paper

8. .... hour and a half

9. .... last person in that line

10. .... ant farm

My score: ____ **10**

My time: ....
                        minutes   seconds

Name: .... **Date:** ....

Write the meaning of each word using the prefix to help you.

1. nontoxic ....

2. inflexible ....

3. autobiography ....

4. microchip ....

5. disconnect ....

6. preview ....

7. dishonest ....

8. multiuse ....

9. semiannual ....

10. impossible ....

My score:
10

My time: ....
minutes   seconds

Minute 88

Name: .... Date: ....

Add a suffix from the box to each root word to create a new word.

| -some | -ness | -tion | -less | -able |

1. dark ....

2. fascinate ....

3. narrate ....

4. thought ....

5. worthy ....

6. restless ....

7. comfort ....

8. sense ....

9. weary ....

10. agree ....

My score: $\dfrac{}{10}$

My time: ....
minutes   seconds

Name: .... **Date:** ....

Draw a line from the Greek or Latin root word to its meaning.

1. pod   far away

2. chrono   time

3. tele   write

4. bio   life

5. derm   build

6. struct   sun

7. scrib   skin

8. sol   right

9. terra   foot

10. just   earth

My score: ___ / 10

My time: ....
                    minutes   seconds

Minute 90

Name: .... Date: ....

For Questions 1–5, cross out the word that is spelt incorrectly.

1. (a) relieve   (b) cieling   (c) brief

2. (a) conceit   (b) vein   (c) frieght

3. (a) mischief   (b) peirce   (c) neither

4. (a) sieze   (b) cashier   (c) deceive

5. (a) conceive   (b) nieghbour   (c) weird

For Questions 6–10, write C if the word is spelt correctly. If the word is spelt incorrectly, write the correct spelling of the word on the line.

6. monkies   ....

7. trolleys   ....

8. poppies   ....

9. spys   ....

10. bays   ....

My score: _____
10

My time: ....
minutes   seconds

Minute 91

Name: .... **Date:** ....

Draw a line through unnecessary negative words. Write another word on the line to replace it if needed.

1. That new restaurant on High Street will not get no business. ....

2. Nobody travels on that road barely at all. ....

3. It won't get hardly no business because it's too secluded. ....

4. They didn't even put no signs out to let people know they are there! ....

5. My family and I ate there once, and there weren't no other customers there but us. ....

6. Nobody thought the food was not delicious. ....

7. Mr Anderson said he thought the restaurant wouldn't stay in business neither. ....

8. The owner said she didn't need no help advertising. ....

9. She wasn't putting up no billboards because they're expensive. ....

10. She hardly had no money for the advertising budget. ....

My score: ___
10

My time: ....
minutes   seconds

Apply your grammar knowledge

Name: .... **Date:** ....

For Questions 1–8, draw a line from each part of speech to its definition.

1. verb		(a)	modifies a verb, adjective, or other adverb
2. noun		(b)	takes the place of a noun
3. adjective		(c)	modifies a noun
4. adverb		(d)	expresses strong feeling
5. conjunction		(e)	joins words or groups of words
6. interjection		(f)	names a person, place, or thing
7. preposition		(g)	shows how two things are related
8. pronoun		(h)	tells the action in a sentence

For Number 9, circle the examples of adverbs.

9. always   unappetising   frustrate   really   startle

For Number 10, circle the examples of prepositions.

10. under   tomorrow   too   to   west

My score: _____
10

My time: ....
            minutes   seconds

www.prim-ed.com   Prim-Ed Publishing®

Name: .... **Date:** ....

Insert punctuation marks (commas, apostrophes, quotation marks and end punctuation) for each sentence.

1. Would you like to dance

2. Look out for that cricket ball

3. I did my homework already

4. Jason please don't interrupt

5. Martie said You are a good actor

6. Please get eggs milk and cereal from the shop

7. Mr Wall cant make his appointment with Dr Smith

8. Oops I dropped my ice-cream cone

9. Clean your room Mum commanded

10. Do you always watch that show

My score:

10

My time: ....
minutes   seconds

Minute 94

Name: .... **Date:** ....

For Questions 1–5, circle the misused word and write it correctly on the line.

1. Did you're sister make the volleyball team? ....

2. There going to Gracetown for a tournament on Saturday. ....

3. You look ill. Would you like to lay down? ....

4. Your going to do well on that test! ....

5. Please sit the post on that desk. ....

For Questions 6–10, insert the correct punctuation at the end of each sentence. Then write the type of sentence it is on the line. Write D for declarative, I for interrogative, IMP for imperative or E for exclamatory.

6. Where should we go for dinner.......... ....

7. We should go to Market City Restaurant for dinner.......... ....

8. Bring cash, because the restaurant doesn't accept credit cards.......... ....

9. I wish I could order two pieces of the cheesecake for dessert.......... ....

10. I can't believe how much I just ate.......... ....

My score: ────
10

My time: ....
minutes   seconds

Minute 95

Name: ....   **Date:** ....

Circle singular, plural, singular possessive *or* plural possessive *to describe the noun in* **bold type** *in each sentence.*

1. Renee loves to watch the **horses** run and play.

    singular   plural   singular possessive   plural possessive

2. The young **foal** follows its mother everywhere.

    singular   plural   singular possessive   plural possessive

3. Two playful **ponies** whinny and snicker.

    singular   plural   singular possessive   plural possessive

4. The **ponies'** movements are swift and graceful.

    singular   plural   singular possessive   plural possessive

5. That **horse's** mane is braided.

    singular   plural   singular possessive   plural possessive

6. **Snowflake's** stall has been cleaned out.

    singular   plural   singular possessive   plural possessive

7. Snowflake will have a new **colt** soon.

    singular   plural   singular possessive   plural possessive

8. Renee used to exercise Snowflake on the **trails** behind the house.

    singular   plural   singular possessive   plural possessive

9. She also keeps the barn stocked full of carrots, the **animals'** favourite treat.

    singular   plural   singular possessive   plural possessive

10. The magnificent **stallion's** coat is shiny and black.

    singular   plural   singular possessive   plural possessive

My score: _____   **My time:** ....

10   minutes   seconds

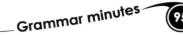

Minute 96

9
8
7
6

Name: .... Date: ....

For Questions 1–5, circle adjective or adverb to describe the words in bold type in each sentence.

1. Jana **sharply** scolded the child for running into the street.

    adjective   adverb

2. 'The cars come **fast**, and they can't see you!' she admonished.

    adjective   adverb

3. The **sheepish** child hung his head.

    adjective   adverb

4. Then he looked at Jana with **teary** eyes.

    adjective   adverb

5. Jana could see that he felt **embarrassed**.

    adjective   adverb

For Questions 6–10, underline the verb and write past, present or future on the line to describe when the action takes place.

6. Trina helps her sister get dressed.   ....

7. Dad had called to see if Aunt Sue was okay.   ....

8. Marie has packed for her camping trip.   ....

9. Matthew will get a puppy by the end of the week.   ....

10. Kelly went to the supermarket for groceries.   ....

My score: _____
10

My time: ....
          minutes   seconds

www.prim-ed.com   Prim-Ed Publishing®

Name: ....   **Date:** ....

Circle **simple, compound, complex** *or* **compound-complex** *to describe the structure of each sentence.*

1. Sir Frank Whittle was a famous inventor.

    simple   compound   complex   compound-complex

2. Benjamin Franklin was an inventor, but he was also a statesman.

    simple   compound   complex   compound-complex

3. He invented things that improved people's lives.

    simple   compound   complex   compound-complex

4. Some inventors are not even trying to invent anything, but they stumble onto a brilliant idea out of necessity or by accident.

    simple   compound   complex   compound-complex

5. When an ice-cream vendor ran out of dishes at the World's Fair, he used rolled-up wafers from a neighbouring stall to make ice-cream cones.

    simple   compound   complex   compound-complex

6. People loved the idea, and they probably always will!

    simple   compound   complex   compound-complex

7. Some inventions make life much easier.

    simple   compound   complex   compound-complex

8. The internet has made research and access to information very simple.

    simple   compound   complex   compound-complex

9. Alfred Bernhard Nobel was a Swedish chemist who held 355 patents for inventions.

    simple   compound   complex   compound-complex

10. Alexander Graham Bell invented the telephone.

    simple   compound   complex   compound-complex

My score: _____ **10**

My time: ....
                        minutes   seconds

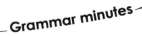

Minute 98

Name: .... Date: ....

Circle the dependent clause in each sentence. Then write complex *or* compound-complex *after each sentence.*

1. Mr Bert loves to work in the flower garden, but he doesn't get to enjoy it very often because he spends so much time at work.

....

2. If he neglects the shrubs, they become bushy and look messy.

....

3. Though Mr Bert usually prefers colourful roses, he planted some fragrant gardenias, and he enjoyed them very much.

....

4. Sometimes, Mr Bert puts off weeding the garden, so he has lots of work to do when he finally gets around to it.

....

5. Mr Bert sits on the patio that is located in his garden.

....

6. All kinds of creatures visit Mr Bert's garden because he places birdbaths and feeders in strategic locations.

....

7. Bees often feed on the honeysuckle, and Mr Bert's children love to watch them as the furry insects buzz from flower to flower.

....

8. Mr Bert also grows herbs in his garden, and Mrs Bert uses them when she is cooking special meals.

....

9. Mr Bert wants his children to garden, though they don't seem interested.

....

10. Mr Bert thought his garden looked nice, but his neighbours, who were impressed with his gardening talents, thought it was spectacular.

....

My score: ___ / 10

My time: ....
          minutes   seconds